A+ books

Animals, Animals!

DO WHALES HAVE WHISKERS?

A Question and Answer Book about Animal Body Parts

by
Emily James

raintree
a Capstone company — publishers for children

Raintree is an imprint of Capstone Global Library Limited, a company incorporated in England and Wales having its registered office at 264 Banbury Road, Oxford, OX2 7DY – Registered company number: 6695582

www.raintree.co.uk

myorders@raintree.co.uk

Text © Capstone Global Library Limited 2017

Edited by Jaclyn Jaycox
Designed by Juliette Peters
Picture research by Jo Miller
Production by Laura Manthe

ISBN 978 1 4747 2790 7 (hardcover)
20 19 18 17 16
10 9 8 7 6 5 4 3 2 1

ISBN 978 1 4747 2794 5 (paperback)
21 20 19 18 17
10 9 8 7 6 5 4 3 2 1

BRITISH LIBRARY CATALOGUING IN PUBLICATION DATA
A full catalogue record for this book is available from the British Library.

PHOTO CREDITS
Newscom: imageBROKER/Bernd Zoller, 14; Shutterstock/Alberto Loyo, 1, back cover, Artush, 22, Audrey Snider-Bell, 10, Eric Isselee, 28 (bottom), Erwin Niemand, 32, Ethan Daniels, 26, JGA, 16, jurra8, 4, Lightspring, 27 (top), Mr. SUTTIPON YAKHAM, 28 (top), Neil Burton, 18, Ondrej Prosicky, 8, Roobcio, cover, Sari ONeal, 20, Steve Byland, 24, stockphoto mania, 27 (bottom), Vladimir Melnik, 12, Wang LiQiang, 6

Design Elements
Shutterstock: Nebojsa Kontic, Olegusk

Printed in China.

DO WHALES HAVE WHISKERS?

No! Seals have whiskers.

whiskers

Seals have long, wavy whiskers. Their sensitive whiskers can feel vibrations in the water. The vibrations tell the seals the size and shape of other animals in the water.

DO WHALES HAVE BEAKS?

No! Parrots have beaks.

beak

Parrots have sharp, curved beaks. Their powerful beaks can break open the hard shells of seeds and nuts. Parrots' beaks can be very colourful. Sometimes they are bright red or flaming orange.

DO WHALES HAVE FEATHERS?

No! Owls have feathers.

Owls have soft, fluffy feathers. Special feathers soften the swooping sound of the owl's wings. Hunting owls can fly silently through the forest and sneak up on their prey.

DO WHALES HAVE LEGS?

No! **Centipedes have legs.**

Centipedes crawl quickly, searching for food at night. A centipede's body is divided into parts. Each part has a pair of long, skinny legs. Centipedes can have as many as 177 pairs of legs.

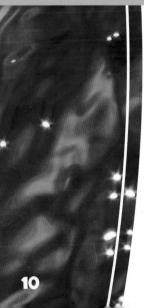

DO WHALES HAVE TUSKS?

No! Walruses have tusks.

tusks

A heavy walrus glides gracefully underwater. But it isn't so easy for the walrus to climb out. The walrus uses its long, sharp tusks to pull its big body up onto an ice floe.

DO WHALES HAVE PAWS?

No! Puppies have paws.

Puppies with big paws often grow into large dogs. Dogs that pull sledges in the snow have very furry paws. These sledge dogs often wear soft booties to protect their paws from ice and snow.

DO WHALES HAVE CLAWS?

No! Lobsters have claws.

claws

Lobsters crawl on the floor of the ocean, waving their heavy claws. One claw is strong enough to crush a crab shell. The other claw has sharp teeth that can tear the crabmeat.

DO WHALES HAVE HORNS?

No! Bulls have horns.

horns

Bulls grow hard, heavy horns on the tops of their heads. A bull's horns are longer and sharper than a cow's horns. As a bull grows bigger, its horns curve and spread apart.

DO WHALES HAVE WINGS?

No! Butterflies have wings.

veins

Monarch butterflies have four strong wings that flutter and flap. Thick, black veins keep their orange wings stiff. These butterflies fly thousands of kilometres to be in a warm place for the winter.

DO WHALES HAVE TRUNKS?

No! Elephants have trunks.

trunk

An elephant's long trunk is much more than a nose. Elephants suck water into their trunks. They spray it into their mouths to drink. Elephants also use their trunks to gather food and greet each other.

DO WHALES HAVE SHELLS?

No! Tortoises have shells.

shell

A tortoise has a hard shell around most of its body. The shell acts like a shield and protects a tortoise from predators. Many tortoises can hide their heads and legs inside their shells.

DO WHALES HAVE FINS?

Yes! Whales have fins.

fluke

flipper

Whales have fins and flippers for turning and splashing. They have flukes on their tails for zooming along, leaving bubbly trails.

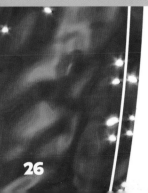

Animal bodies

Some animals have bright, colourful bodies.

brilliant wings ⟶ monarch butterflies

flashing beaks ⟶ parrots

monarch
butterfly

Some animals have bodies that
blend in with their surroundings.

dark as deep water ⟶ walruses

walrus

tortoise

Some animals have hard bodies.

thick shells ⟶ lobsters

crunchy skin ⟶ centipedes

strong frame ⟶ tortoises

Some animals have soft bodies.

smooth, hairy skin ⟶ bulls

fuzzy fur ⟶ puppies

fluffy feathers ⟶ owls

waterproof coat ⟶ seals

Some animals' bodies are too big to hide!

heavy hulks ⟶ whales

giant creatures ⟶ elephants

owl

GLOSSARY

beak the hard, front part of a bird's mouth

fin flap sticking out from the back of the bodies of some whales. Whales use their fins for moving steadily through water.

flipper wide, flat flap sticking out from the side of a whale's body that it uses for swimming and steering

floe large sheet of floating ice

fluke the wide, flat end of a whale's tail

predator animal that hunts other animals for food

prey animal that is hunted by another animal for food

protect keep safe

shield object that gives protection from harm

stiff hard to bend or turn

tusk one of two very long, pointed teeth that curve out of the mouths of some animals such as walruses

vein small, stiff tube that helps a butterfly's wing keep its shape

vibration fast movement back and forth

whale large animal that lives in the ocean. A whale looks like a fish but is actually a mammal that breathes air.

COMPREHENSION QUESTIONS

1. How many wings does a monarch butterfly have? What colour are they?

2. Tortoises have hard shells that help keep them safe from predators. What is a predator?

3. Name one body part you have. What does it help you do?

READ MORE

Mammal Body Parts (Animal Body Parts), Clare Lewis (Raintree, 2015)

Ocean Animals (Creature Crafts), Annalees Lim (Wayland, 2015)

Why Do Monkeys and Other Mammals Have Fur? (Animal Body Coverings), Holly Beaumont (Raintree, 2015)